D1621546

EASY COMFORT FOOD

EASY COMFORT FOOD

MUD PUDDLE BOOKS, INC.

NEW YORK

EASY COMFORT FOOD

Copyright © 2004

By Sheryn R. Jones

All rights reserved.

Published by

Mud Puddle Books, Inc.

54 West 21st Street

Suite 601

New York, New York 10010

info@mudpuddlebooks.com

ISBN: 1-59412-016-1

All rights reserved. No part of this book may be reproduced or transmitted in any form or by any means, electronic or mechanical, including photocopying, recording, or by any information storage and retrieval system, without permission in writing from the publisher.

Printed in China

Designed by Elizabeth Elsas

TABLE OF CONTENTS

EASY COMFORT FOOD FOR DESSERT

U.S. MEASUREMENT AND METRIC CONVERSION CHART

Here is a simple chart that makes conversion from U.S. measurements to metric as easy as pie.

1 TEASPOON	5 ML
2 TEASPOONS	10 ML
1 TABLESPOON	15 ML
2 TABLESPOONS	30 ML
1 CUP	237 ML
2 CUPS = 1 PINT	473 ML
3 CUPS	710 ML
4 CUPS = 1 QUART	95 LITER
4 QUARTS = 1 GALLON	3.8 LITERS
1 OUNCE	28 GRAMS
2 OUNCES	57 GRAMS
3 OUNCES	85 GRAMS
4 OUNCES	113 GRAMS
6 OUNCES	170 GRAMS
8 OUNCES	227 GRAMS
16 OUNCES = 1 POUND	454 GRAMS
2.2 POUNDS	1 KILOGRAM

U.S. MEASUREMENT TO METRIC CONVERSION FORMULAS

TO CONVERT:	MULTIPLY WHAT YOU KNOW BY:
CUPS TO LITERS	x .236
CUPS TO MILLILITERS	x 236.6
GALLONS TO LITERS	x 3.8
OUNCES (FLUID) TO MILLILITERS	x 29.6
OUNCES (WEIGHT) TO GRAMS	x 28.4
PINTS TO LITERS	x .47
POUNDS TO KILOGRAMS	x .45
QUARTS TO LITERS	x .95
TABLESPOONS TO MILLILITERS	x 14.8
TEASPOONS TO MILLILITERS	x 4.9

INTRODUCTION

Comfort Food . . . it is an inner hug . . . a good feeling . . . a "fix" for days gone by.

In the South, "comfort food" means someone is fixin' to fix dinner because the kids are fixin' to come home. Just as grandma's bread pudding smoothed the feathers from a sibling spat years ago, today the same classic dessert can take us away from a world of depositions, performance evaluations, traffic tickets and salary negotiations.

Ah, the comfort foods we love . . . Chicken-fried steak nestled under a blanket of pepper-speckled cream gravy . . . green bean casserole next to creamy mashed potatoes . . . and the sweet, tart taste of your favorite cherry pie . . . How much better can it get?

Easy Comfort Food captures all the favorite comfort foods we had growing up. Our collection captures the special memories that go with the family table, meals at a friend's house, casseroles from church suppers, after-school treats and holiday standards.

When round pegs have square holes and two plus two keeps coming up five, it is soothing to know that Cheerleaders' Brownies or Mom's Spaghetti and Meatballs can make it all better. Maybe we cannot alter strategies or change events, but a favorite comfort food can put us in sync with a life at full throttle.

Enjoy this collection of *Easy Comfort Food*. It is guaranteed to bring a little warmth, a little happiness and a lot of memories to your table. So take a quick trip back to your youth, back to simpler days and simpler ways.

GOOD MORNING COMFORT FOOD

♉ WESTERN OMELLETE

6 eggs
6 tablespoons milk
½ cup grated cheddar cheese
½ cup diced cooked ham
¼ cup finely chopped onion
¼ cup finely chopped green peppers
    or chopped green chilies, drained
¼ cup chopped tomatoes
Salsa

Beat eggs with milk. Over medium heat melt butter in omellete pan or skillet and pour one half the eggs into pan. Tilt pan or use spoon to move liquid of eggs around pan to cook evenly. Cook until eggs are almost firm in the middle. Sprinkle cheese, ham, onion, green peppers and tomatoes over one half the eggs. Fold other half of omellete over to cover cheese mixture and continue cooking 1 or 2 minutes longer or until eggs are firm and cheese melts. Slide out of pan, pour salsa over top and serve immediately.

♉ BACON-CHEESE OMELLETE

2 strips bacon
2 eggs
1 tablespoon milk
2 green onions with tops, chopped
1 tablespoon butter
½ cup grated cheddar cheese

Fry bacon crispy, drain, cool and crumble. Sauté onion in remaining bacon drippings and drain. Beat eggs with milk. Over medium heat melt butter in omellete pan and pour in egg mixture. Tilt pan or use spoon to move liquid of eggs around pan to cook evenly. Cook until eggs are almost firm in center. Sprinkle bacon, onions and cheese evenly over half of eggs. Fold one half of omellete over to cover cheese and continue cooking 1 or 2 minutes until cheese melts. Serve immediately.

FRENCH TOAST

2 eggs
1 cup milk
1 tablespoon sugar
1 teaspoon vanilla or ground cinnamon
1 tablespoon butter
6 to 8 slices white bread
Powdered sugar
Maple syrup

Beat eggs, milk, sugar and vanilla or ground cinnamon. Heat griddle until butter melts. Dip both sides of bread into milk-egg mixture. Cook on both sides until brown. Remove from griddle and sprinkle with powdered sugar or maple syrup.

CRISPY FRENCH TOAST:

Crispy French Toast has a crust or coating on outside that makes it crispy. Use ½ cup flour in batter to make crust. Cook until crispy.

Note: Many kinds of breads may be used for French Toast. Possibilities include Texas toast about one-inch thick, or challah or French bread cut in thick slices.

Basic Pancakes

2 cups flour
1 tablespoon sugar
1 tablespoon baking powder
¼ teaspoon salt
2 eggs
1½ to 2 cups milk, divided
Vegetable oil
Maple syrup
½ cup melted butter

Combine flour, sugar, baking powder and salt in large mixing bowl. In separate bowl, beat eggs and 1½ cups milk. Pour egg mixture into flour mixture and stir until smooth. If batter is too thick, add a little milk. There will be a few lumps in batter. Heat griddle and coat lightly with oil. Slowly pour circle of batter on griddle to equal desired size of pancake. After bubbles form on top and edges brown, gently flip pancake to cook other side. Serve immediately with warm syrup and melted butter.

BLUEBERRY PANCAKES:

Wash and drain thoroughly about 1 cup fresh or frozen blueberries. (If blueberries are frozen, do not thaw before adding to pancake batter.) Stir into pancake batter gently and pour onto griddle or skillet.

BUTTERMILK PANCAKES:

Substitute buttermilk instead of milk. If batter is too thick, add just a little milk.

BANANA PANCAKES:

Slice 1 or 2 ripe bananas about ¼-inch thick. When batter is poured onto griddle, place as many slices as desired on batter and lightly push bananas into batter. Cook slowly to make sure inside is firm.

Note: Other variations include apples, cranberries, coconut, bacon, ham and pecans.

❧ Buttermilk Waffles

2 eggs, separated
2 tablespoons oil
2 (1 pint) cups buttermilk
2¼ cups flour
1½ teaspoons baking powder
½ teaspoon baking soda
½ teaspoon salt

Beat egg yolks with oil and add buttermilk. Combine dry ingredients and add to buttermilk mixture. In separate bowl beat egg whites until stiff peaks form. Slowly fold into batter. Bake in preheated waffle iron until crispy brown.

❧ Crispy Waffles

2 cups biscuit mix
1 egg
½ cup oil
1⅓ cups club soda

Preheat waffle iron. Combine biscuit mix, egg, oil and club soda in mixing bowl and stir by hand until well blended. Pour just enough batter to cover waffle iron and cook about 5 to 7 minutes until golden brown.

BISCUITS AND SAUSAGE GRAVY

3 cups biscuit mix

¾ cup milk

½ pound ground, pork sausage

¼ cup (½ stick) butter

⅓ cup flour

3¼ cups milk

½ teaspoon salt

½ teaspoon pepper

Preheat oven to 400°. To make biscuits combine biscuit mix and milk in medium bowl and stir to mix. Put wax paper on counter top and sprinkle lightly with flour. Roll out dough to ¾-inch thick and cut out circles with floured cookie cutter or drinking glass. Put on sprayed baking sheet and bake for 12 to 15 minutes or until golden brown. Cook sausage in skillet and drain drippings except for about 1 to 2 tablespoons. Add butter to drippings and melt. Add flour and cook 1 minute, stirring constantly. Gradually add milk and cook over medium heat, stirring constantly, until gravy thickens. Stir in seasonings and crumbled sausage or serve sausage on the side. Serve gravy immediately and pour over biscuits.

EASY COMFORT FOOD FOR LUNCH

Old-Fashioned Tomato Soup

2½ pounds fresh tomatoes, peeled,
   seeded, chopped or 4 cups canned
   stewed, chopped tomatoes
3 to 4 cups chicken stock
2 ribs celery, minced
1 carrot, minced
1 onion, minced
2 tablespoons basil
Salt
Pepper
Lemon juice

In large soup pot, combine tomatoes, chicken stock, celery, carrot, onion and basil on high heat. After soup begins to boil, reduce heat to low and simmer for 15 to 30 minutes. Add basil, salt and pepper to taste. Use fresh lemon juice, a little at a time, and taste.

CREAM OF TOMATO SOUP:

Omit chicken stock and onion and substitute 2 to 3 cups half-and-half cream. Bring to almost boiling and reduce heat to simmer.

CHICKEN-NOODLE SOUP

Chicken stock
1 (3-4 pound) whole chicken
1 carrot, chopped
2 ribs celery with leaves, chopped
½ to ¾ cup egg noodles, cooked
Salt
Pepper

Wash whole chicken and giblets and put in large soup pot. Add 7 to 8 cups water, carrot and celery and bring to boil. Reduce heat and simmer, partially covered, for 30 minutes to 1 hour or until meat is tender. Remove chicken from soup pot and cool. Continue simmering and spoon off fat from top of liquid when needed. Bone chicken and put all bones and skin back into soup pot. Continue to simmer for 3 to 4 hours. Turn heat off and strain chicken stock in large bowl. Add chopped chicken and cooked egg noodles. Salt and pepper to taste.

CHICKEN SOUP WITH RICE:

Omit noodles and add 1½ tablespoons uncooked rice to chicken stock. Cook until rice is done.

❧ Caesar Salad

1 (1.2 ounce) package Caesar salad dressing
½ head romaine lettuce
¼ cup shredded parmesan cheese
Croutons

Tear lettuce in small pieces. Pour on Caesar salad dressing and toss. Add shredded parmesan cheese and croutons. Chill before serving.

❧ Cobb Salad

2 to 3 boneless, skinless chicken breast halves
6 slices bacon
½ head iceberg lettuce
½ head romaine lettuce
1 avocado, peeled, pitted, diced
3 hard-boiled eggs, diced
2 green onions with tops, chopped
2 tomatoes, peeled, diced
¾ cup shredded, sharp cheddar cheese
1 ounce crumbled roquefort cheese
Salad dressing of choice

In large saucepan boil chicken breast halves in enough water to cover for 30 to 40 minutes. Cool and dice. Fry bacon crispy, drain, cool and crumble. Tear iceberg and romaine lettuce in small pieces and toss together in salad bowl. Arrange each ingredient in its own area on top of lettuce: one area for chicken, one for bacon, one for avocado, one for eggs, one for onion and one for tomatoes. Sprinkle with both cheeses or arrange them in their own areas. Chill before serving. Serve with favorite dressing.

Tuna Fish Salad

1 (12 ounce) can tuna fish, drained
½ cup chopped celery
¼ cup chopped pecans
2 hard-boiled eggs, finely chopped
¼ teaspoon onion salt
Mayonnaise

Drain tuna and put in medium bowl. Add celery, pecans, eggs, onion salt and enough mayonnaise to moisten mixture. Chill and serve.

Chicken Salad

6 to 8 boneless, skinless chicken breast halves
½ cup chopped celery
½ cup chopped onion
2 hard-boiled eggs, diced
6 tablespoons mayonnaise
Salt & Pepper

In large saucepan boil chicken breast halves in enough water to cover for 30 to 40 minutes. Cool, dice chicken and place in large bowl. Add onion, celery, eggs and mayonnaise and mix well. Salt and pepper to taste. Spread on favorite bread, mound on lettuce leaves or stuff in hollowed out tomato.

Egg Salad

4 hard-boiled eggs
⅓ cup mayonnaise
1 tablespoon Dijon mustard
1 rib celery, minced
Salt & Pepper

Mash eggs with fork and stir in mayonnaise, mustard and celery. Add salt and pepper to taste. Spread on bread and serve as sandwiches.

GRILLED CHEESE SANDWICHES

Butter
Bread
American, cheddar or Velveeta cheese slices

Butter 1 side of bread slice and put in hot skillet over medium-high heat. Add cheese over bread and put another bread slice, buttered on 1 side, on top. Cook 2 to 3 minutes for cheese to melt and bread to brown. Flatten sandwich slightly with spatula. If bread slices stick together, turn sandwich with spatula and brown other side. When second is brown, serve immediately.

Note: Add some of the following ingredients for a change: ham slice, lunch meat slice, cooked, crispy slices of bacon, thin slices of tomato, jalapenos, thin slices of onion, mozzarella cheese, parmesan cheese, sharp cheddar cheese, Monterey Jack cheese and Swiss cheese.

Potato Salad

6 large potatoes
1 hard-boiled egg, chopped
1 medium onion, chopped
½ bell pepper, chopped
2 ribs celery, chopped
¼ cup sweet pickle relish, drained
1 large dill pickle, chopped
Salt & Pepper
1½ teaspoons mustard
½ cup mayonnaise

Peel and wash potatoes, cut each potato in 4 to 6 pieces and put in large saucepan. Cover with water and boil until potatoes are tender. Cool and cut potatoes into bite-size pieces. Stir together cubed potatoes, egg, onion, bell pepper, celery, pickle relish, dill pickle, salt, pepper, mustard and mayonnaise and mix well. Chill and serve.

Cole Slaw

½ cup mayonnaise
1 teaspoons vinegar
⅛ teaspoon salt
⅛ teaspoon white pepper
⅛ teaspoon sugar
Dash Worcestershire sauce
1 small head cabbage
1 small carrot, shredded
½ bell pepper, sliced thinly

Mix mayonnaise, vinegar, salt, white pepper, sugar and Worcestershire sauce in small bowl and set aside. (It may be necessary to double these to cover cabbage.) Shred or slice cabbage into very thin slices and put in medium bowl. Add carrot and bell pepper and toss. Add mayonnaise mixture to cabbage and toss until cabbage is coated with dressing.

EASY COMFORT FOOD FOR DINNER

✒ Spaghetti and Meatballs

Meatballs:

2 pounds lean ground round
½ pound ground pork
4 eggs
2 cups grated Italian cheese
1½ cups dry French breadcrumbs, rolled fine
1 onion, chopped
2 cloves garlic, pressed
½ bunch fresh parsley, minced
½ cup milk
1½ tablespoons ketchup
Salt & Pepper
Olive oil

Toss all ingredients lightly and shape into balls. Brown in olive oil and set aside.

Sauce:

1 onion, minced
1 clove garlic, pressed
1 tablespoon olive oil
2 (6 ounce) cans tomato paste
1½ to 2 quarts water
Salt & Pepper
1 tablespoon minced sweet basil
1 tablespoon ground oregano

In heavy saucepan sauté onion and garlic in olive oil until soft and clear. Add tomato paste, water, salt, pepper, basil and oregano and mix well. Add browned meat balls and simmer for 1 one hour or until sauce thickens. Serve over cooked spaghetti. Serves 6 to 8.

Pot Roast

1 (4 to 5 pound) boneless rump roast

Seasoned salt

Seasoned pepper

Garlic powder

2 cups water

6 medium potatoes, peeled, quartered

8 carrots, peeled, quartered

3 onions, peeled, quartered

Preheat oven to 375°. Place roast in roasting pan with lid and sprinkle liberally with salt, pepper and garlic powder. Add 2 cups water and bake covered for about 30 minutes. Lower heat to 325° and bake covered for 3 hours. Add potatoes, carrots and onions. Bake another 35 to 40 minutes. Lift roast from pan and place on serving dish. Arrange potatoes, carrots and onion around roast.

GRAVY:

3 tablespoons cornstarch

¾ cup water

½ teaspoon pepper

½ teaspoon salt

Combine cornstarch and water and pour into juices in roaster. Add pepper and salt. On stove burner, cook juices on high and stir constantly until gravy thickens. Serve in gravy boat with roast and vegetables. Serves 8.

☙ MEATLOAF

1½ pounds ground round

1 teaspoon salt

1 egg

½ cup milk

1 cup crushed breadcrumbs

½ cup chopped onion

1 (6 ounce) can tomato paste

Preheat oven to 325°. In large bowl mix ground round, salt, egg, milk, breadcrumbs, onion and tomato paste. Form meat mixture to loaf. Place in sprayed 9 x 9- inch baking dish. Bake 50 to 60 minutes.

Variations:

Add ½ cup grated cheese to meat mixture.

Instead of using all ground round, use half ground round and half ground pork.

Add slice of bacon on top before cooking.

Add tomato sauce.

TOMATO SAUCE:

2 tablespoons olive oil

¾ cup tomato paste

2½ cups canned, chopped stewed tomatoes

1 teaspoon sugar

5 tablespoons butter

Salt

Pepper

In heavy saucepan over medium heat, heat oil and stir in tomato paste, stewed tomatoes, sugar and butter. Simmer for about 30 minutes. Add salt and pepper to taste. Pour over meatloaf during last 15 minutes of cooking or serve on the side.

❧ TURKEY AND DRESSING/STUFFING

1 (15 to 18 pound) turkey
Salt
Pepper
1 cup butter, softened

Put turkey in refrigerator to thaw 3 to 4 days before cooking. When ready to cook, remove metal clamp from legs. Run cold water into breast and neck cavities until giblets and neck can be removed. (Interior should be cold to slightly icy.) Refrigerate until ready to cook.

To cook turkey, preheat oven to 325º. Rub entire turkey with butter and lightly salt and pepper. Place turkey in roaster, breast side up. Cover bottom of pan with ½ to 1 cup water. Place 1 or 2 ribs celery and ½ peeled white onion inside the cavity. Cover with lid or foil. Follow cooking time chart and baste occasionally with drippings while turkey is cooking.

COOKING TIMES FOR TURKEY:

Weight of turkey	Cooking time at 325º
6 to 8 pounds	3 to 3½ hours
8 to 12 pounds	3½ to 4½ hours
12 to 16 pounds	4½ to 5½ hours
16 to 20 pounds	5½ to 6½ hours
20 to 24 pounds	6½ to 7 hours

DRESSING:

The same recipe can work for dressing or stuffing. Dressing is usually a side dish prepared in a baking dish and stuffing is put inside the cavity of the bird. Both are great and tradition usually determines how it is served.

2 (7.5 ounce) boxes cornbread mix

9 biscuits

1 small onion, chopped

2 ribs celery, chopped

2 eggs

Pepper

2 teaspoons poultry seasoning

3 (14 ounce) cans chicken broth, divided

Before making dressing, prepare cornbread and biscuits according to package directions. Preheat oven to 350°. Crumble cornbread and biscuits into large bowl using a little more cornbread than biscuits. Add onion, celery, eggs and seasonings. Stir in 2½ cans chicken broth. If mixture is not "runny", add rest of broth. (If it is still not runny, add a little milk.) Bake in sprayed 9 x 13-inch glass baking dish at 350° for about 45 minutes or until golden brown. (This may be frozen uncooked and thawed just before cooking.)

GRAVY:

2 (10 ounce) cans chicken broth, divided

2 heaping tablespoons cornstarch

Giblets from turkey

Salt

Pepper

2 hard-boiled eggs, sliced

To make gravy, mix cornstarch with ½ cup chicken broth and stir until there are no lumps. Add remaining broth, giblets, salt and pepper and cook on medium for about 1 hour, stirring frequently, until giblets are done and broth thickens. Remove giblets, chop finely and put back in gravy. Add boiled eggs, pour in gravy boat and serve.

GOULASH

1 cup uncooked macaroni
1½ pounds ground chuck
5 tablespoons chili powder
1 (15 ounce) can tomato sauce
1 cup shredded colby cheese

In medium saucepan bring 3 cups water to rapid boil. Slowly add macaroni and cook on low until tender. In large skillet brown ground chuck and drain. Add chili powder, tomato sauce and cooked macaroni to meat in skillet. Simmer on low heat for 30 minutes. Garnish with shredded cheese. Add more chili powder if you prefer zestier flavor.

CHICKEN POT PIE

6 to 8 skinless, boneless chicken breast halves
¼ cup (½ stick) butter
2¼ cups biscuit mix, divided
1½ teaspoons salt
½ teaspoon pepper
2 (10 ounce) cans chicken stock, divided
⅔ cup whipping cream or half-and-half
½ cup milk

Note: If you want to do this like grandmother made it, bake a whole chicken and strain juices to make chicken stock.

Bake or boil chicken breasts until tender, cool and cut into pieces. Preheat oven to 350º. In small saucepan melt butter and stir in ¼ cup biscuit mix, salt and pepper. Remove from heat and stir in all but 3 tablespoons chicken stock, cream and chicken. Cook over low heat about 5 minutes until mixture thickens. In separate bowl mix remaining 2 cups biscuit mix, remaining 3 tablespoons chicken stock and milk vigorously with fork. Spread wax paper on counter and sprinkle with flour. Knead dough 8 to 10 on wax paper. Pat or roll dough to fit top of 4 to 5 individual baking dishes or 9 x 9-inch baking pan. Pour hot filling into baking dish, cover with dough and bake about 15 minutes or until top is golden brown.

♀ GRILLED PORK CHOPS

4 (1 inch) thick center-cut pork chops
2 to 3 tablespoons olive oil
2 tablespoons fresh lemon juice
Salt
Pepper
1 lemon

Start charcoal fire or heat gas grill. Allow pork chops to reach room temperature. When fire is ready, dry pork chops with paper towel and season with olive oil, a little lemon juice and a lot of salt and pepper. Place pork chops on grill and sear both sides for a minute or two to seal the juices inside. Move to cooler part of grill and cook 5 to 10 minutes or until chops are firm to the touch and juices are slightly pink on the inside. (Cooking time will vary with type of fire, thickness of chops and covered and uncovered grill. The main thing is not to overcook which dries out pork chops.) Remove chops from grill, drizzle with a little more lemon juice and serve immediately.

♀ MACARONI AND CHEESE

1 cup uncooked macaroni, divided
¼ cup (½ stick) butter, sliced
1½ cups grated sharp cheddar,
    Colby or Velvetta cheese
⅔ cup milk
Salt
Pepper
Tabasco, optional

Cook and drain macaroni. Stir in butter and mix to melt. Put half macaroni in sprayed, casserole dish. Mix cheese, milk and seasonings and pour half over macaroni. Pour remaining macaroni into dish and cover with remaining cheese mixture. Bake at 350° until brown on top.

FRIED CHICKEN

1 chicken, cut up or 10 to 12 chicken pieces
Salt
Pepper
2 tablespoons cream or milk
2 eggs, beaten
Flour
Oil

Rinse and pat dry each piece of chicken and place on wax paper. Salt and pepper each piece of chicken on both sides. Add cream or milk to beaten eggs and dip chicken in egg mixture. Roll in flour to coat all sides. Heat ¼ inch oil in heavy skillet. Brown chicken on both sides. Lower heat and cook until tender, about 25 minutes. When done, remove chicken and drain on paper towels.

GRAVY:

3 tablespoons flour
½ teaspoon salt
½ teaspoon pepper
1½ cups milk

After all chicken has been fried, add 3 tablespoons flour, salt and pepper to drippings. Stir and turn burner to medium heat. Pour in milk and cook, stirring constantly, until gravy thickens.

 CHILI

2 pounds beef chuck, cubed

2 tablespoons oil

1 onion, chopped

3 cloves garlic, chopped

1 (8 ounce) can tomato sauce

1 cup beef broth

3 to 5 tablespoons chili powder

2 teaspoons ground cumin

½ teaspoon salt

½ teaspoon pepper

Brown beef in hot oil in large, heavy saucepan. Stir in onion, garlic, tomato sauce and beef broth. Stir to mix well. Add chili powder, cumin, salt and pepper and stir to mix. Cover and simmer for 1 to 2 hours and stir occasionally. If liquid is too thin, remove cover and continue simmering.

Note: To make chili hotter, add more chili powder or slices of seeded jalapenos. Add additional seasonings a little at a time, cook 10 minutes and taste.

 BAKED BEANS

1 (1 pound) can pork and beans

4 tablespoons brown sugar

¼ teaspoon dry mustard

¼ cup ketchup

¼ cup chopped green pepper

¼ cup chopped onion

3 or 4 slices bacon, halved

Preheat oven to 350°. Combine beans, sugar, ketchup, onion, green pepper and mustard and mix well. Pour into sprayed, casserole dish and top with bacon. Bake for 1 hour. Serve immediately.

Barbecued Ribs

There are as many dry rubs and barbecue sauces as there are cooks. Here are three from which to choose.

Ribs:

*8 to 10 pounds spareribs, baby back ribs
    or country-style ribs*

Dry Seasoning Rub:

4 tablespoons paprika
2 tablespoons chili powder
1 tablespoon dry mustard
1 teaspoon basil, minced
1 tablespoon meat tenderizer
½ teaspoon cayenne pepper
½ teaspoon onion salt
½ teaspoon garlic salt

Combine all ingredients in medium bowl and mix thoroughly. Rub onto half of ribs and let set for 1 hour before cooking. Use one of the sauces below for the other half of ribs.

Barbecue Sauce:

½ cup oil
1 cup chopped onion
1 cup ketchup

Sauté onion in oil until soft and clear. Add remaining ingredients. Simmer for 30 minutes.
Use sauce on ribs during the last hour of cooking.

⅓ cup fresh lemon juice

3 tablespoons sugar

3 tablespoons Worcestershire sauce

2 tablespoons prepared mustard

2 teaspoons salt

1 teaspoon pepper

on charcoal grill. If you want to cook ribs in the oven, roast them for 4 to 5 hours at 275° or 300° in large, covered roasting pan. Add water if ribs are drying out. Increase cooking time, if necessary, and cook until meat falls off the bones. Makes about 3 cups.

TERIYAKI SAUCE:

¼ cup teriyaki sauce or soy sauce

¼ cup white wine

1 clove garlic, minced

2 tablespoons brown sugar

2 tablespoons Worcestershire sauce

Combine all ingredients. Marinate meat or vegetables. Baste while cooking.

Barbecued Brisket

1 (7 pound) trimmed beef brisket

1 (4 ounce) bottle liquid smoke

½ teaspoon garlic salt

½ teaspoon onion salt

½ teaspoon celery salt

1 teaspoon seasoned pepper

Preheat oven to 350º. Place brisket in large baking pan and coat generously with liquid smoke. Sprinkle spices over brisket and cover pan with foil. Place in refrigerator overnight. When ready to bake, drain about ¾ of liquid smoke from pan.

Sauce:

1 (16 ounce) bottle ketchup

½ cup packed brown sugar

1 teaspoon prepared mustard

1½ teaspoons garlic powder

1 tablespoons Worcestershire sauce

⅛ teaspoon cayenne pepper

¼ cup vinegar

Combine ketchup, brown sugar, mustard, garlic powder, worcestershire, cayenne pepper and vinegar in saucepan. Blend well. Cook over medium heat until mixture thickens. Pour over brisket and cook for 1 hour. Lower heat to 275º and cook for 4 to 5 hours.

❧ MASHED POTATOES

3 to 4 large russet potatoes
¼ cup milk
⅓ cup butter
1 teaspoon salt
1 teaspoon white pepper

Variation: Add 1 teaspoon garlic salt.

Peel, cut each potato into 4 to 6 pieces and boil in medium saucepan until tender. Drain water and pour potatoes into mixing bowl. Cool and cut into small pieces. In mixing bowl, beat potatoes until they are well blended, but still lumpy. Add milk, butter, salt and pepper. Whip potatoes until smooth and creamy.

❧ CREAMY MASHED POTATOES

6 large potatoes
1 (8 ounce) carton sour cream
1 (8 ounce) package cream cheese, softened
1 teaspoon salt
½ teaspoon white pepper

Preheat oven to 325º. Peel, cut up and boil potatoes until tender. Drain water and whip hot potatoes with add sour cream, cream cheese, salt and pepper. Whip until cream cheese melts. Pour in greased 3-quart baking dish. Cover with foil and bake for 20 minutes. Serves 8 to 10.

❧ BROILED STEAK

1 (1-2 inch thick) sirloin or porterhouse steak
Oil
Salt
Fresh ground pepper

Allow steak to come to room temperature. Preheat oven on broil. Lightly oil broiler rack and put in a drip pan. With rack about 4 inches below broiler, cook steak about 3 to 5 minutes on each side for rare and longer for well done.

❧ GRILLED FILET MIGNON

4 (8 ounce) filets
Salt
Fresh ground black pepper

Preheat charcoal or gas grill and clean grate before cooking. When the flames of charcoal fire have turned into a low fire of red hot coals, put filets on grill. Cook 3 to 5 minutes on each side according to taste. If meat is soft, it is rare. If it is firm, it is well done. Season with salt and ground pepper to taste.

CHICKEN-FRIED STEAK AND CREAM GRAVY

½ cup milk

1 egg

¾ cup flour

½ teaspoon salt

¼ teaspoon black pepper

1 (1½ pound) round steak, tenderized

Oil

In small bowl, beat milk and egg. In another small flat bowl, mix flour, salt and pepper. Cut tenderized round steak into 4 to 6 pieces. Coat each cutlet with seasoned flour, dip in milk-egg mixture and coat with seasoned flour again. Press flour into steak during last coating. Pour about 1 inch oil into skillet and heat. When oil sizzles, carefully lay each steak in skillet. Cook on each side until golden brown. Drain on paper towel.

CREAM GRAVY:

¼ cup (½ stick) butter

⅓ cup flour

½ teaspoon salt

½ teaspoon pepper

3¼ cups milk

Drain all drippings except 1 tablespoon from skillet. Add butter and seasonings to melt. Over medium heat stir in ¾ cup milk slowly, stirring constantly, until gravy thickens. Cook until heated thoroughly and serve immediately..

French Fries

4 pounds russet potatoes
Salt
Vegetable oil

Cut potatoes into lengths about ¼ x ¼ x 3 inches. Place in large bowl, cover with water and chill in refrigerator for about 2 hours. Pour oil in deep saucepan to depth of 4 inches and warm over medium heat. Drain potatoes and pat dry with paper towels. When oil begins to sizzle, carefully drop a few potatoes at a time in saucepan and cook about 1 to 2 minutes until crisp and golden. Drain on paper towel and sprinkle with salt. Continue cooking in small batches and serve immediately

French Green Bean Casserole

2 (14.5 ounce) cans French-cut green beans
1 (5 ounce) can water chestnuts
1 (10 ounce) can cream of mushroom soup
2 cups grated sharp cheddar cheese
2 (2.8 ounce) cans French fried onion rings

Drain green beans and water chestnuts. In medium bowl mix green beans and water chestnuts with mushroom soup. Spray 9 x 13 x 2-inch baking dish and pour green bean mixture into dish. Cover with grated cheese and bake at 350º for 15 minutes. Remove from oven and pour French fried onion rings evenly over top of dish. Bake another 15 to 20 minutes until hot throughout and browned on top.

❧ BEEF AND NOODLE CASSEROLE

1½ cups cooked, cubed beef

2 eggs

1 cup sour cream

½ cup grated Swiss cheese

1 onion, chopped

Salt & Pepper

1 (8 ounce) package egg noodles, cooked

Preheat oven to 350º. Use leftover roast and cut in bite-size pieces. In medium bowl, beat eggs slightly and stir in sour cream. Add Swiss cheese, onion, beef and salt and pepper to taste. Butter 2-quart casserole dish and pour cooked noodles evenly over bottom. Pour cheese-beef sauce over noodles and gently toss to mix.

Variations: Omit leftover beef and substitute 1½ cups cooked, chopped chicken or 1½ cups cooked, chopped ham.

❧ CHICKEN-NOODLE CASSEROLE

1 (6 ounce) package noodles, divided

1 (10 ounce) can cream of chicken soup

1 (5⅓ ounce) can evaporated milk

¼ teaspoon salt

1 cup shredded cheddar cheese

3 cups diced, cooked chicken

1 cup diced celery

¼ cup diced pimiento, drained

1 cup slivered almonds, toasted, divided

Toasted, buttered breadcrumbs

Preheat oven to 400º. Cook noodles according to package directions and drain. Place half noodles in each of 2 small, sprayed casseroles or 1 large casserole dish. Combine soup, milk and salt in medium saucepan and heat, stirring constantly. Add cheese and stir until cheese melts. Add chicken, celery, pimiento and half the almonds and stir to mix well. Pour mixture over noodles in casserole dishes. Bake uncovered for about 20 minutes to heat thoroughly.

FRIED FISH

Fish fillets
Corn meal
Salt
Pepper
Oil

Lay fish fillets on wax paper and pat dry on both sides. Pour corn meal into wide-mouth bowl. Sprinkle salt and pepper in corn meal and mix thoroughly. Dip several fish fillets in corn meal mixture and coat both sides. In heavy skillet pour oil to cover half the fish. Heat oil until it bubbles slightly. Carefully slide each fish fillet into skillet. (Be careful not to splash hot oil.) Brown well and turn once. When second side browns, lift from pan and drain on paper towels. Serve immediately.

TARTAR SAUCE:

½ cup mayonnaise
¼ cup India relish, drained

Mix mayonnaise and relish and serve. Amount of relish may vary according to taste.

COCKTAIL SAUCE:

1½ cups cocktail sauce
4 tablespoons lemon juice
3 tablespoons horseradish
2 teaspoons worcestershire
½ teaspoon grated onion
4 drops hot sauce
Salt to taste

Combine all ingredients and chill for several hours.

Party Pizza

1 pound ground sausage

1 (14 ounce) jar pizza sauce

1½ teaspoons oregano

¼ teaspoon garlic powder

1 cup chopped onion

½ cup shredded parmesan cheese

½ cup grated mozzarella cheese

1 (10 inch) pizza crust

In medium skillet cook and drain sausage and set aside. To pizza sauce, add oregano and garlic powder. Spread pizza sauce evenly over pizza crust. Sprinkle sausage, onion, parmesan cheese and mozzarella cheese on top of pizza sauce. (Add additional ingredients according to your own taste.) Bake at 350º until cheese melts and pizza is bubbly on top.

Variations: Add pepperoni slices, ground beef, Canadian bacon slices, green olives, black olives, bell pepper, mushrooms, jalapenos and/or anchovies.

Cheeseburger

1 pound bacon
2 pounds ground beef
Salt
Pepper
8 slices cheese
8 hamburger buns
1 large onion, sliced
Lettuce
Tomatoes
Pickle slices
Mustard
Mayonnaise
Ketchup

Fry bacon and drain drippings from pan. Mix ground beef and salt and pepper and form into 8 patties. Cook on charcoal grill or in skillet until almost done. Add cheese slice on top of meat. Allow cheese to melt and put meat on warm bun. Add bacon, onions, lettuce, tomatoes and pickles. Dress with mustard, mayonnaise and/or ketchup.

CALIFORNIA BURGERS:

Replace ground beef with ground turkey. Use bean sprouts, avocado slices and tomatoes instead of bacon, onions, lettuce and pickles.

WESTERN BURGERS:

Replace raw onion with sautéed onion, sautéed fresh mushrooms and add chili sauce, hickory sauce or ketchup.

SOUTHWESTERN BURGERS:

Use green chili salsa and grated Mexican, four-cheese blend.

PINEAPPLE-GLAZED HAM

1 (7 pound) shank or butt-end ham
Whole cloves
1 (14 ounce) can chunk pineapple, drained

Preheat oven to 350°. Stick whole cloves on the outside of ham. With toothpicks stick pineapple chunks on ham.

SAUCE:

1 cup red wine or cooking wine
1 cup packed brown sugar
1 tablespoon cut-up crystallized ginger
1½ teaspoons dijon mustard
1 (8 ounce) can crushed pineapple

In saucepan, combine wine, brown sugar, crystallized ginger, mustard, crushed pineapple and bring to boil. Remove from heat. Place ham in roasting pan and pour hot sauce over ham. Cook for 10 to 15 minutes per pound. Baste with sauce every 20 minutes.

EASY

COMFORT

FOOD FOR

DESSERT

♫ Peach Cobbler

3 cups sliced fresh peaches

1 tablespoon lemon juice

¼ teaspoon almond extract

1 cup sifted flour

1 cup sugar

½ teaspoon salt

1 egg, beaten

6 tablespoons butter, melted

Preheat oven to 375º. Butter 10 x 6-inch baking dish. Place peaches on bottom. Sprinkle with lemon juice and almond extract. In separate bowl, sift flour and add sugar and salt. With fork stir in eggs and mix until crumbly. Sprinkle over peaches and drizzle with melted butter. Bake 35 to 40 minutes.

Oatmeal Cookies

1 cup packed brown sugar

1 cup granulated sugar

1 cup vegetable shortening

2 eggs

2 cups flour

1 teaspoon baking soda

1 teaspoon baking powder

½ teaspoon salt

2 cups old-fashioned oats

1 cup chopped nuts

1 cup raisins

1 teaspoon vanilla

Preheat oven to 350°. Cream sugar and shortening in mixing bowl. Add eggs and mix well. Sift together flour, baking soda, baking powder, salt and add to sugar mixture. Stir in oats, nuts, raisins and vanilla. Roll in 1-inch balls. Bake on ungreased cookie sheet for 8 to 10 minutes. Makes 8 dozen.

Variation: Add 1 cup flaked coconut.

Toll House Chocolate Chip Cookies

2¼ cups unsifted all-purpose flour

1 teaspoon baking soda

1 teaspoon salt

1 cup butter, softened

¾ cup sugar

¾ cup firmly packed brown sugar

1 teaspoon vanilla

2 eggs

1 (12 ounce) package semi-sweet,
real chocolate morsels

1 cup chopped nuts

Preheat oven to 375°. Combine flour, baking soda and salt in medium bowl and set aside.

In large bowl combine butter, sugar, brown sugar and vanilla extract and stir until creamy. Add eggs and mix thoroughly. Add flour mixture a little at a time and stir to mix well. Add chocolate morsels and nuts and mix. Drop by rounded teaspoonfuls onto ungreased baking sheets. Bake for 8 to 10 minutes. (The longer the cookies bake, the crispier they will be.)

Apple Pie

7 apples, peeled, cored, sliced
½ teaspoon lemon juice
½ cup packed brown sugar
1 (9-inch) double pie crust
¼ cup butter, sliced
1 teaspoon cinnamon
¼ cup sugar

Preheat oven to 400º. In large bowl, combine sliced apples, lemon juice and brown sugar and cinnamon. Pour in prepared pie shell and dollop with butter. Place second pie crust on top of apples and pinch sides to seal. Cut small slits in top pie crust. Sprinkle with sugar. Bake for 30 to 40 minutes or until crust is golden brown.

Cherry Pie

4 cups pitted, red tart cherries
1¼ cups sugar
¼ cup flour
¼ teaspoon cinnamon
2 tablespoons butter

Preheat oven to 425º. Prepare crust for 1 (9-inch) pie pan with 2 pie crusts. In large bowl, lightly stir cherries and sugar together. Stir in flour and lemon juice. Spoon into pie pan with bottom crust. Dot with butter and place top crust over pie filling. Fold edges of top crust under edges of bottom crust to seal. Flute edges with fingers. Cut several slits in top crust. Bake for 15 minutes and remove pie from oven. Cover edges of pie crust with foil to keep them from burning. Return to oven and bake for 20 to 25 minutes or until pie is bubbly and crust is golden brown.

ℒ PUMPKIN PIE

4 slightly beaten eggs

2 cups canned or mashed cooked pumpkin

1 cup sugar

½ cup dark corn syrup

1 teaspoon vanilla

½ teaspoon cinnamon

¼ teaspoon salt

1 (9-inch) unbaked pie shell

Mix all ingredients and pour into pie shell. Bake at 350° for 40 minutes or until firm in center.

ℒ BREAD PUDDING

1 (1-pound) loaf raisin-cinnamon bread

4 tablespoons butter, softened

4 eggs, beaten

1 cup sugar

1 teaspoon vanilla

¼ teaspoon salt

3 cups scalded milk

Preheat oven to 350°. Cut sliced bread into cubes. Place in buttered, 3-quart baking dish. Beat eggs, sugar, vanilla and salt until blended. Stir in hot milk and pour over bread. Allow mixture to set until bread cubes absorb liquid. Gently mix and bake for 50 to 55 minutes or until set.

Variations: Add fresh blueberries or raisins to give a little more flavor.

The Ultimate Brownie

⅔ cup butter

5 (1 ounce) squares unsweetened baking
   chocolate, chopped

1¾ cups sugar

2 teaspoons vanilla

3 eggs

1 cup flour

1 cup chopped nuts

Chocolate Frosting

Preheat oven to 350°. Melt butter and chocolate in saucepan over low heat, stirring constantly. Beat sugar, vanilla and eggs in medium bowl at high speed 5 minutes. Beat in chocolate mixture at low speed. Beat in flour until blended. Stir in nuts. Spread in 9 x 9-inch sprayed baking pan. Bake 35 to 40 minutes or until brownies pull away from sides of pan. Cool and spread with Chocolate Frosting. Cut into squares.

Chocolate Frosting:

4 tablespoons butter

2 ounces unsweetened baking chocolate

2 cups powdered sugar

4 tablespoons hot water

Melt butter and chocolate in saucepan over low heat, stirring constantly. Remove from heat and stir in powdered sugar and hot water to spreading consistency.

CHEERLEADERS' BROWNIES

⅔ cup oil

⅓ cup corn syrup

½ cup cocoa

½ teaspoon salt

1 cup chopped nuts

2 cups sugar

4 eggs, beaten

1½ cups flour

1 teaspoon baking powder

2 teaspoons vanilla

Preheat oven to 350°. In large bowl combine oil, sugar, corn syrup and eggs and mix well. In separate bowl, mix cocoa, flour, salt and baking powder. Pour flour mixture into sugar-egg mixture, a little at a time, mixing after each addition. Add vanilla and nuts and beat well. Pour into greased, floured 7 x 11-inch baking pan and bake at 350° for 45 minutes or until toothpick inserted in center comes out clean. (Do not overcook.) Serve immediately.

CRUNCHY PEANUT BUTTER BROWNIES

1 cup (2 sticks) butter

2 cups sugar

6 tablespoons unsweetened cocoa

2 teaspoons vanilla

4 eggs

1 cup flour

½ teaspoon salt

Topping (page 62)

Preheat oven to 350°. In mixing bowl, cream butter, sugar, cocoa and vanilla until smooth. Add eggs, one at a time, and beat well after each addition. Fold in flour and salt. Spread mixture in sprayed 9 x 13-inch baking pan. Bake at 350° for 25 minutes. Remove from oven and cool.

TOPPING FOR CRUNCHY PEANUT BUTTER BROWNIES

1 (7 ounce) jar marshmallow cream
1 cup chunky or smooth peanut butter
1 (12 ounce) package chocolate chips
3 cups crispy rice cereal

After brownies have cooled, spread marshmallow cream evenly over top of brownies. In large heavy saucepan over low to medium heat, melt peanut butter and chocolate chips together, stirring constantly. Remove from heat and fold in crispy rice cereal. Spoon peanut butter-chocolate mixture over marshmallow cream and spread evenly. Chill several hours, cut into squares and serve.

SNICKER BROWNIES

1 (18 ounce) box German chocolate cake mix
¾ cup (1½ sticks) butter, melted
½ cup evaporated milk
4 (2.7 ounce) Snicker candy bars

Preheat oven to 350º. In large bowl combine cake mix, butter and evaporated milk. Beat on low speed until well blended. Pour half the batter into greased, floured 9 x 13-inch baking pan. Bake at 350º for 10 minutes. Cut Snicker bars in ⅛-inch slices. Remove from oven and place candy bar slices evenly over brownies. Drop remaining half of batter by spoonfuls over candy bars and spread as evenly as possible. Return to oven and bake for 20 minutes longer. Cool and cut into squares.

Chocolate Pound Cake

1 cup (2 sticks) butter, softened

2 cups sugar

1 cup packed brown sugar

6 large eggs

2½ cups flour

¼ teaspoon baking soda

½ cup cocoa

1 (8 ounce) carton sour cream

2 teaspoons vanilla

Preheat oven to 325º. Grease and flour 10-inch tube pan. Combine in mixing bowl, butter, sugar and brown sugar. Beat with electric mixer about 2 minutes until soft and creamy. Add eggs, beating well. Combine flour, baking soda and cocoa; add to creamed mixture alternately with sour cream and vanilla, beginning and ending with flour mixture. Mix at lowest speed just until blended after each addition. Spoon batter into tube pan and bake for 1 hour and 20 minutes or until toothpick inserted in center of cake comes out clean. Cool in pan for 10 to 15 minutes. Remove from pan and cool on wire rack.

Cheesecake

2 (8 ounce) packages cream cheese, softened

3 eggs

½ cup sugar

½ teaspoon almond extract

½ pint sour cream

2 tablespoons sugar

1 teaspoon vanilla

Preheat oven to 350º. Blend cream cheese, eggs, sugar and almond extract. Pour into pie shell and bake 30 minutes. Remove from oven and reduce heat to 300º. Mix well sour cream, sugar and vanilla. Pour into sunken shell. Bake at 300º for 10 minutes.

Toppings: Cheesecake may be served by itself or with toppings such as cherry pie filling, blueberry pie filling, fresh strawberries, fresh blueberries or lemon sauce.

Carrot Cake

4 eggs
2 cups sugar
1⅓ cups oil
2 cups flour
1 teaspoon salt
2 teaspoons baking soda
2 teaspoons baking powder
2 teaspoons ground cinnamon
3 to 4 cups grated carrots
¾ cup chopped pecans

Preheat oven to 325°. Combine sugar and eggs and beat well. Sift flour, salt, baking soda, baking powder and cinnamon together. Add to sugar mixture a little at a time and alternately with oil. Add carrots and nuts. Bake in 3 (8-inch) greased and floured, layer cake pans. Bake for 45 minutes. Remove from oven to cool and frost with Cream Cheese Icing.

Cream Cheese Icing:

½ cup (1 stick) butter, softened
1 (8 ounce) package cream cheese, softened
1 (16 ounce) box powdered sugar
1 teaspoon vanilla
1 cup chopped nuts

Beat butter and cream cheese. Add powdered sugar and vanilla and beat to mix well. Spread over 3 layers, top and sides of cooled cake.

Strawberry Shortcake

1 quart strawberries
Sugar
2 cups biscuit mix
¾ cup milk
3 tablespoons melted butter
2 tablespoons sugar

Wash and stem strawberries. Slice diagonally into a medium bowl. Pour enough sugar to cover strawberries. Cover bowl with plastic wrap and chill for several hours. The longer the strawberries chill, the more juice in the bowl.

Preheat oven to 450°. Combine biscuit mix, milk, butter and 2 tablespoons sugar until all biscuit mix is blended with other ingredients. Spread wax paper on counter and lightly dust with flour. Knead dough on wax paper about 8 to 10 times. Roll dough to ½-inch thickness. Cut with floured 3-inch, round cookie cutter or drinking glass with sharp edge. Bake on ungreased baking sheet about 10 minutes or until golden brown on top. When ready to serve, slice shortcakes in half, pour strawberries over bottom half, top with whipped topping and pour more strawberries and whipped topping on top if desired.

℘ CHOCOLATE CUPCAKES

3 cups flour

2 cups sugar

½ cup cocoa

2 teaspoons baking soda

1 teaspoon salt

2 cups water

⅔ cup oil

2 tablespoons vinegar

1 teaspoon vanilla

Mix all ingredients well. Put cupcake papers in muffin tins and fill papers half full of batter.

1 (8 ounce) cream cheese, softened

1 unbeaten egg

½ cup sugar

⅛ teaspoon salt

1 cup chocolate chips

Preheat oven to 350º. Mix cream cheese, egg, sugar and salt and beat well. Stir in chocolate chips. Put generous tablespoon of batter on top of each cupcake. Bake for 25 minutes. Makes 3 dozen.

Hot Fudge Sundae

1 cup semi-sweet chocolate chips
1 tablespoon butter
¼ cup sugar
½ cup evaporated milk

In heavy saucepan over low heat, melt chocolate, butter and sugar, stirring constantly. Remove from heat, pour in milk and stir until smooth. In separate bowl, place 1 or 2 scoops vanilla ice cream, pour hot fudge over top, sprinkle nuts, whipped topping and maraschino cherry on top. Serve immediately.

Variations: Variations are numerous and here are just a few ideas.
Put a brownie in the bowl with ice cream, hot fudge sauce, nuts, whipped topping and cherry on top.
Slice fresh strawberries, cover with sugar and chill for 3 or 4 hours. Pour strawberries and juice on top.
Try any of the following coconut, heated peanut butter, butterscotch sauce, caramel sauce, pineapple sauce, 10 or 12 halved maraschino cherries and cherry juice, chopped candy bars and cookies crumbs.

Banana Split

1 firm banana
1 scoop each: vanilla, chocolate,
    strawberry ice cream
2 tablespoons each: chocolate syrup,
    strawberry syrup, butterscotch sauce
Whipped cream
Maraschino cherries
2 tablespoons chopped nuts

Peel banana and slice in 2 pieces lengthwise. Put 1 scoop each of vanilla, chocolate and strawberry ice cream between slices of banana. Pour chocolate syrup, strawberry syrup and butterscotch sauce over scoops of ice cream. Top with whipped cream, maraschino cherries and nuts.